NO EXCUSES!

Your Guide to Successful Authorship

JENNIFER SHARP

Copyright © 2020 Jennifer Sharp

First published in Australia in 2020

MMH Press

www.mmhpress.com

All rights reserved. No part of this book may be used or reproduced by any means, graphic, electronic, or mechanical, including photocopying, recording, taping or by any information storage retrieval system without the written permission of the copyright owner except in the case of brief quotations embodied in critical articles and reviews.

Cover design: Carolyn De Ridder

National Library of Australia Cataloguing-in-Publication data:

Non-Fiction – self-help/personal growth/success

Non-Fiction – small business/growth/success

No Excuses: Your Guide to Successful Authorship/
Jennifer Sharp

ISBN: 978-0-6488253-1-9 (sc)

ISBN: 978-0-6488253-2-6 (e)

To Karen

Thank you for always believing, especially when I didn't believe in myself.

CONTENTS

Introduction: ……………………………………….1

Chapter 1: Where Do I Begin?...............................7

Chapter 2: Negative and Positive Mindsets………15

Chapter 3: Mindset Challenges…………………...21

Chapter 4: Affirmations…………………………...33

Chapter 5: Where do I Find the Content?................39

Chapter 6: Setting Smart Goals…………………...59

Chapter 7: Dreams Do Come True………………..65

Chapter 8: Marketing and Self-Care………………71

INTRODUCTION

"If the book is true, it will find an audience that is meant to read it."
Wally Lamb

Why Write A Book?

This book has been written to support those of you who want to write your story. Maybe you have words of wisdom to impart, or you want to grow your business. Maybe you have a vivid imagination and write as a form of escapism. For most of us we struggle at the beginning – we don't know where to start – or is that an excuse? Whatever struggle you think you may have with penning your story, I offer many tips and techniques to get you on your way. No excuses accepted.

How many of you have made the following excuses?

- ✓ *I'm too busy.*
- ✓ *There's no time.*
- ✓ *I have to cook dinner*
- ✓ *I work all day.*

- ✓ *Friends are coming over for lunch.*

- ✓ *The in-laws have arrived.*

- ✓ *Got to walk the dog.*

Then there are those fixed mindset issues:

- ✓ *I'm not good enough.*

- ✓ *No one would read my work.*

- ✓ *I don't know enough about the subject.*

- ✓ *I don't know where to start.*

- ✓ *I just can't. I don't know enough.*

How many times have you spoken the above words? Yes, it takes time, and effort. Yes, you need to walk the dog, and go to your day job. Yes, you need to cook dinner and visitors do disrupt the routine. You also need to stop making excuses. You can write, you can find the time, you do know how to research, you are good enough.

Just Begin.

It's your choice.

If you are ready to write your story, if you are ready to stop making excuses, if you're ready to discard the words above, then this is the book for you.

My word for this year is ACTION, and that's what I want you to take. This isn't a read in the park book. It's a get off your butt and stop making excuses Action book. My goal is to help you find your Why, and to establish your content, which you most likely already have. Just have a look at your Facebook, LinkedIn posts. How many of you have been interviewed or do interviews? Do you podcast? Create You Tube videos? Write articles for newspapers? If so, you already have your story, and most importantly, your audience.

Be accountable for yourself by setting intentions. Daily or weekly intentions to keep you on track, to move you forward step by step. Setting intentions keeps your mind clear and focused about what you need to do and helps to shift the mindset from that of a fixed one (I can't) to one of I can! (growth).

Do you believe in yourself? I believe in you. Are you ready to get out of your own way? Are you ready to commit to you? Are you ready to Action your dream?

Only you can make it happen. With a little nudge from me. The world needs to hear your story.

Welcome to NO Excuses.

Jennifer

CHAPTER ONE

Begin at the beginning and go on till you come to the end; then stop." Lewis Carroll

Where do I begin?

At the beginning.

Often the writer's dilemma comes with having too many ideas. What do you do with them all? You can't let them getaway. But then, this idea doesn't gel with that one and so forth. This is also an excuse. Your thoughts, ideas, may not be totally clear. You might perceive them as being some kind of blockage within you, your mind.
Then it all gets too hard.
Your first strategy – Know your Why. Understand it 100%.
This is mine.

My Why began many years ago as a little girl. Each Sunday when I visited my grandparents, I would climb into my grandfather's arms and he would read me a story.

I don't recall what he read but I will always remember how his voice sang with each word spoken. He taught me that you could be and do anything if you could read, had an education, and that words empower no matter who you are or where you come from. My grandfather wasn't educated, leaving school at 12, learning to read at 14. I was only 8 when he passed.

Teaching in the early years enabled me much access to books and watching children learn and grow with them. And then, when I was coaching and mentoring within the Education Department, I found even more value in books which led me to writing my own. It was a natural progression for me to leave teaching and turn to publishing, always with my grandfather's words in mind.

What is my Why?

- All children have the right to be able to hold and read a book.
- All children have the right to an education.
- All words inform and inspire, empower, and educate the reader regardless of who they are.

Know your why. 100%. Ask yourself the following questions:

- Why do you want to write your story?
- What is the point of it?

- How will this book change your life, or better still, someone else's?

- Is it going to make the reader laugh, cry or both?

- What other emotions might it invoke?

- Will the reader resonate so strongly with it they can't wait to share it or try what you have suggested?

Visualise your Why. Draw it. Can you fully see it? Commit to it. Action it.

Draw your Why.

Spend time thinking about the above points. Answer them on the lines below or on a separate sheet of paper.

What are you going to do to action them? NO Excuses accepted.

Why do you want to write your story?

_____
_____
_____
_____

What is the point of it?

_____
_____
_____
_____

How will writing this book change your life or someone else's?

_____
_____
_____
_____

Is your book going to make the reader laugh, cry or both?

_____
_____
_____
_____
_____

What other emotions might it invoke?

_____
_____
_____
_____
_____

Will the reader resonate so strongly with your words they can't wait to share it?

_____
_____
_____
_____
_____

Will the reader want to try what you have suggested?

_____

_____

_____

_____

_____

Know your Why 100% and commit to it.

Believe it.

Believe in you.

Commit to writing like you do eating three meals a day. If you live it – breath it, you are a writer, and people will want to hear your story.

CHAPTER TWO

"Keep your face to the sunshine
and you cannot see the shadow."
Helen Keller

Negative and Positive Mindsets

What mindset do you have?

The following four questions have been adapted from Dr Carol Dweck's book, Mindset – Changing The Way You Think to Fulfil Your Potential (2017). Answer with a Yes or No.

1. Do you think you can't change your intelligence? _____

2. Can you learn new things but accept your intelligence is the same? _____

3. You know you are intelligent but that you can also change it? _____

4. You understand you can continuously learn at all times? _____

If you answered yes to the first two questions, you are working within a *fixed* mindset.

If you answered yes to the last two questions you are working within a *growth* mindset.

If you think within a fixed mindset framework, you will most likely have negative thoughts continually circling inside your mind about yourself and your capabilities. All those *I can't because* thoughts.

If you think within a growth mindset framework, you know you can continually learn. Your mind will continually circle with *I can do it* thoughts regardless of how many times you try. You know with continued perseverance and grit you will accomplish your goal.

Let's discuss some of those negative, fixed mindset objections:

- *I'm not good enough.*
- *I can't.*
- *Why would anyone want to read my book?*
- *I don't have time.*
- *It's too hard.*

Do you remember all those? And there are so many more.

Looking at your answers to the previous questions, do these fixed mindset objections still exist in your vocabulary? Yes? No? Why? Write down your answers and explain them.

_____
_____
_____
_____
_____
_____
_____
_____
_____
_____
_____
_____
_____
_____
_____
_____

Ask yourself the following questions and any others that may cross your mind:

- *Do you want to be asked as a speaker to events?*
- *Do you want to build credibility as an author, as an expert in your field?*
- *What do you want to get out of being a published author?*
- *Do you want a passive income to offset your day job?*
- *Do you want to build up a readership, so writing becomes your day job?*
- *Do you want to grow your writing business?*

When we give serious thought to what's stopping us from writing, when we sift through all the internal blockages, it's not the penning of words that is the difficulty. It's all those underlying excuses that resurface. All those - *I'm not good enough's, no one will want to read my book* – excuses that creep back in. This is when you need to stay focused with that positive mindset.

Do you still want to publish a book? Answer the following questions.

- ✓ *Are you willing to persevere through it?*
- ✓ *Do you have enough grit to get through it?*
- ✓ *Are you ready to commit to yourself?*

NO Excuses.

Let's begin.

CHAPTER THREE

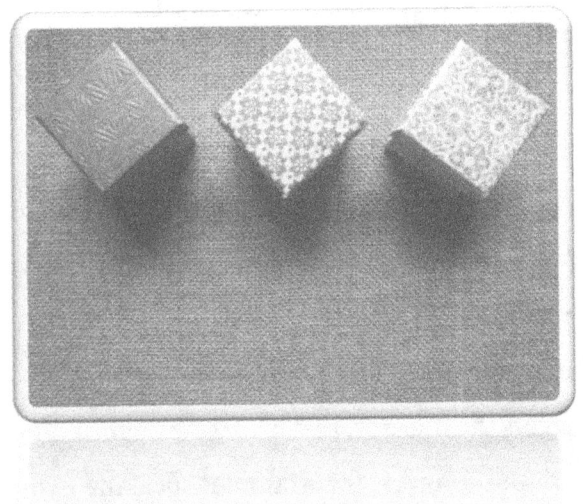

"No matter what, people grow. If you chose not to grow, you're staying in a small box with a small mindset. People who win go outside of that box. It's very simple when you look at it."
Kevin Hart

Mindset Challenges

Hopefully by now you've established and understand your Why 100% and you are prepared to work within a growth mindset. You've identified why you want to write your book and how it can move you and others forward in your careers, businesses, and life. New opportunities may appear in the form of, for example, speaking events and presenting workshops, and new doors to experiences you would never have imagined are now opening for you.

It's time to work on your mindset.

You may still have some fears, doubts, lack of confidence - *I'm not good enough, I'm not an expert* - thoughts circling inside your mind. Are these real doubts, fears? Or, are they still being used as excuses?

As a mindset coach, I often hear these words. As a writer, I confess, I am guilty of saying them to myself at times when writing in a different genre. Are they excuses or are they genuinely real thoughts for the person feeling them? Most of the time, we perceive them as being real. Children present with both fixed and growth mindsets and as an educator it was my job to nurture the growth mindset for continued learning. But for adults with a fixed mindset, it's much more difficult to do. Speaking generally, as adults, we have spent many years perfecting the negative, especially when referring to ourselves and our capabilities.

How do we unlock the negatives, the blockages, as adults to support each other, particularly in writing? When coaching and mentoring clients, I need to unlock what it is in their past that has created these blockages, these *I can't* perceptions of themselves. All these issues negatively impact your writing, your self-belief in writing a book. Fear is the biggest block for anyone and not just for writing. Fear stops us from living life fully in so many ways. Many writers simply shut down, giving up before they even try.

I've seen and heard highly successful business owners, those who are at the top of their game, fall apart. They sit at their desks, turn on their computer, or take out pen and paper, then stare blankly. They have the content, they know what they want to write, but the words won't come.

Shut down has begun. Shut down happens every time they sit to do this task.

Next, all the excuses begin - *Best walk the dogs now. Think I need a coffee. Do I need to get anything out of the freezer for dinner? I wonder if there's laundry to do?... Another day is over. I'll write tomorrow. There's no time anymore today, must return that phone call...*

These excuses are all based on Fear Factors –
- *The Imposter Syndrome.*
- *The I'm not good enough syndrome.*
- *What if no one wants to read my book syndrome?*
- *What if no one wants to buy my book? They know I'm not an expert (even though I've been doing it for 20 years) syndrome.*
- *I'll never be a success syndrome.*

These all stem from having a negative, fixed mindset. Sometimes it's easier to stay in our comfort zones than it is to stretch ourselves to our full potential.

Let's turn these above negative points into positive, growth mindset statements:

- ✓ *I'm not an imposter – I KNOW my stuff.*
- ✓ *I AM good enough.*
- ✓ *Everyone WILL want to read my book.*
- ✓ *My book will be IN DEMAND. Everyone wants to buy it.*
- ✓ *I've been doing this for years. I think I've learnt a few things along the way. I am an EXPERT in my field.*
- ✓ *I will be a GLOBAL success.*

What are you fearing? Write each fear down.

_____

_____

_____

_____

_____

_____

_____

_____

What are you celebrating? Write each celebration down.

_____

_____

_____

_____

_____

_____

_____

We all face these struggles from time to time. Its human nature. But it's important to not let fear rule your beliefs, especially belief in yourself and your capabilities. Open your mind to Growth. What's the worst that can happen?

Now, it's your job to celebrate your fears. Yes, you read correctly. Celebrate them. Write them down. Re-read through the fears you wrote above. Look at the words you wrote. Breathe them in then breathe them out. Take them for what that are. NO more excuses. NO more what if's.

If you do this, you will gradually change your mindset. Negative thoughts will eventually turn to positive. Take

Action. *I cant's* will become *I Can's. What if's* will become *I Did, I Am, I've got this.* You've kicked fear in the butt! How do you feel now?

Its only when your mindset changes to what it is you can do, when you acknowledge your capabilities, that you can move forward with writing your book. You've slayed the Fear Monster instead of it slaying you.

Now, there are a few things I want you to do. Make a list of all the negatives in your life that affect what you do. Rule a line down the middle of a page and on the left side at the top write negative thoughts or draw a sad face or whatever you want to do to express negativity. Write down all the negative thoughts you have each day whether it be about writing or life in general. This list may be long, or it could be short. It's your list and yours alone.

On the right side of the page, write at the top, positives. Walk your eyes down the negatives one at a time and reverse it. For example, you might have *I don't speak well* on the left. On the right this will change to *I am the best speaker ever!* Alternately, complete the following pages.

By doing this and focusing on the positives you are re-wiring you brain. You are changing it from a fixed - *I can't do anything* - mindset to a growth - *I am learning and I can do* - mindset. Use the positives as affirmations each morning.

Give yourself ten minutes each morning for a week to write down all the negatives in your life and in particular, regarding writing. Then give yourself 15 minutes each morning for a week to write down their opposites. Fill this in over the page or get another sheet of paper if you feel the need.

Negatives	Positives

Focusing on the positives only, give yourself permission to action each one of them. Write one down each day and action it. Make a daily commitment and stick to it.

Today I will …

_____

_____

Today I will …

_____

_____

Today I will …

_____

_____

Today I will …

_____

_____

Today I will …

_____

_____

The last thing I want you to do is to accept the positives and give yourself permission to use them. It's one thing to write them down and acknowledge them, but you must Action them if you are going change your thinking.

I give myself permission to believe in myself as a writer. I acknowledge my fears and strengths with writing. I acknowledge I now have a positive mindset and 100% know why I want to write this book and who will read it.

From today onwards I will Action this.

I've got this!

Date: _____

CHAPTER FOUR

"Am I good enough?
Yes, I am." Michelle Obama

Affirmations

Say it every day and it will be.

Getting out of bed one day and deciding on the spot that today is the day you believe in yourself to write your book is the first step toward taking Action. But, very quickly those negative thoughts may creep back in and by morning tea you'll be saying – I'll start tomorrow.

Deciding that today is the day is wonderful. But you need to constantly repeat the positives you discovered in the previous chapters to affirm your intention. Say them over and over, out loud each morning and night with conviction. You must believe in yourself and your words.

An affirmation is a short, powerful statement, that helps you train your mind and believe in what you intend to Action.

If you want negativity in life, keep having negative thoughts. Those *I'm not good enough, I can't* thoughts.

If you want positivity in life, keep having positive thoughts - *I CAN do this. People WILL want to read my story.*

Do not let fear get in your way. Fear equals – I can't write that book because I'm not good enough.

Turn that into a positive affirmation. *I am an expert in my field and people will want to know my story.*

State your affirmations out loud –

- ✓ *I am a writer.*
- ✓ *I am an expert in my field.*
- ✓ *People will want to read my book.*

Let's take Action on your writing affirmations.

List one fear you have about yourself as a writer then change it into a positive statement. Begin with five affirmations then grow the positives as you become more confident in yourself. Repeat your affirmations morning and night. Say them out loud and with full intent.

Write them down on the following page.

Fear:

_____

_____

Positive Affirmation:

_____

_____

Fear:

_____

_____

Positive Affirmation:

_____

_____

Fear:

_____

_____

Positive Affirmation:

_____

_____

Fear:

_____

_____

Positive Affirmation:

_____

_____

Fear:

_____

_____

Positive Affirmation:

_____

_____

Fear:

_____

_____

Positive Affirmation:

_____

_____

Fear:

_____

_____

Positive Affirmation:

_____

_____

Fear:

_____

_____

Positive Affirmation:

_____

_____

Mindset challenges will always be with you throughout your writing process. At times you will feel anxious, unworthy, like you are running out of time, don't have enough content, family issues will kick in and so forth. These words are just that Fear Monster trying to sabotage you. Those feelings are real. Acknowledge them, breathe them in then let them go. Otherwise, they will take over your thoughts again and your thought patterns will go back to the negativity.

If, and when this happens, keep reaffirming with yourself that all will be okay. Restate clearly your affirmations, commit to yourself and them. It's time to keep moving forward.

You CAN do this!

You CAN write your book!

CHAPTER FIVE

"Make your vision so clear that your fears become irrelevant."

Nibedita Singh

Where Do I Find The Content?

Inside of you.

Many of you will already have all the content you need stored inside your mind. Now it's time to retrieve it.

So, pick up your pen and just begin. Yep, that's all you've got to do. A great big brain dump. Don't worry about the order of contents, your grammar, lack of punctuation. That will all come. Just let the words flow down from your internal retrieval system, through your arm and onto paper. Much research indicates the strongest link for writing is to use the hand – brain connection for initial thoughts and writing. The keyboard can come later. However, this is optional. Write how you wish to write. Just get going!

But, it's not that easy, right?

When speaking with clients about writing a book and the benefits it can bring, especially if it a book about their business, I am more often than not, faced with the author asking – Where do I start? I'm not sure what to write about?

These are words spoken by those who are at the top of their game. All their expertise goes down the drain as they fall apart at writing a few words on paper. This is natural. Its normal. They go through that *imposter syndrome* meandering. It's amazing how penning a few words can be so intimating.

Books are an important tool for what you do. To share your knowledge and expertise globally. There are so many people who will benefit from your message, and your story just may help them move forward in their lives and businesses. Believe in yourself and others will too. Even on the rough days.

Firstly, what I find useful to do, and many others do also, is to mind map your story. Pick up your pen and draw an outline. Visualise your book. Think about how it will look and feel. Mind maps help you see your story, piece by piece, chapter by chapter. Mind maps help you to organise and categorise each chapter, they give you snapshots of what each chapter will look like and the chapters in total. This, in turn, shows you what your finished book will look like.

Mind maps can be big or small, plain or colourful – whatever you want them to be. They are visual reminders to you, that support you, in staying focused with your story. They help you to chunk down your content, rearrange it, play with it until you get the structure you want for your chapters to flow smoothly. The more you map your writing, the easier the words will flow.

Mind maps can lead you into places you didn't know existed or you didn't want to go to, and that's okay. Go with the flow; with what's easiest for you. What comes most naturally to you. If it comes naturally to you, your vision will become clearer, your words will be authentic, and you will have absolute clarity. Clarity stems from having a well-defined vision.

Mind map example 1:

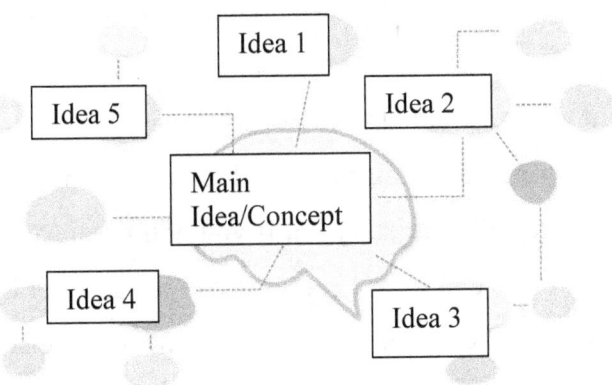

Keep your chapter outline simple: focus on the major points you want to share with the world. Then keep chunking down. Brainstorm each key idea, write down each key point in dot form, then expand on it. Most of all, believe in yourself. Know the world needs to hear your story.

What does *chunking down* mean? When I was teaching the term *chunking it* was often referred to as breaking down the content in the curriculum. When you chunk something down, you are simply breaking everything down into manageable parts, piece by piece, chapter by chapter, paragraph by paragraph, sentence by sentence.

Once you have completed your book outline – chunk it down more. This helps you to see clearer what your end result will look like. Visualise it. Re-draw your mind map. Visual representation is great to see how all the chunks fit into the final product. It's also fun to do. Get someone to help you with it; to help you and your ideas flow. This brings so much clarity to what you do know and shows you where you might need to go.

You may have all the knowledge and expertise in the world to sell your story but if you don't believe in yourself, no one else will. People need to see and feel who you truly are. They need to know they can have a relationship with you. They need to be able to trust you. This will show in your words.

It's doesn't matter how many degrees you may have, what research you have done, what data you may have collected, how many years experience you have, if you haven't written what you know from your heart, your readers will see right through you.

Draw your own mind map. Google mind maps if nothing comes to mind for you. There is a huge amount to choose from.

Look at your mind map. List all the reasons why people will want to read, or need to read, your book.

_____
_____
_____
_____
_____
_____
_____
_____
_____

List your current network of people who support you.

_____
_____
_____
_____
_____
_____
_____
_____
_____

Commit to yourself, your support network, and your readers. By this, I mean commit to writing each day – it doesn't matter if it's for 15 minutes in the morning or 15 minutes at night. It's making the commitment that is important. Get into the habit of it. Like exercising your body, brushing your teeth, eating 3 meals a day – make it a routine accomplishment.

Give yourself a timeline. Choose a date for when you'd like to do a book launch. Tell your network. They can all be your accountability buddies. Do you want your launch to coincide with a special day? Highlight that date then work backwards. There are no particular rules for when or where you can have a launch. You just need to make sure you leave yourself enough time to reach that particular goal.

Make that commitment. Say it out loud. Write it out.

I will commit to writing my book.

_____

_____

State out loud your positive affirmations completed in previous chapters.

Fill in the following:

It will take _____ hours per week of writing to complete my first draft.

It will take _____ weeks/months from editing to publication.

My estimated launch date will be
_____.

You may be thinking by now this is all too hard. Be assured, you can do it. NO, you are not too busy, too tired, too hungry; too whatever. Keep kicking that Fear Monster.

If you are ready to share your story, make writing a priority in your life. You've made your commitment. Stick to it. Believe it. Believe in yourself. Take Action and achieve it.

You're running a business, you've worked in the same profession for years, you are continuously asked questions, you perhaps, coach or mentor others. How many times have you answered the same questions over and over, in small groups, in staff meetings, in emails. You have probably written articles for journals, newspapers, blog posts around the content you are answering every day. Am I right?

When you're in meetings, write down the common thread of questions asked. Is there a theme? While you are doing this begin to create topic-based content with the questions and your answers. These become your framework – your chapters. Use them to your advantage.

Your potential clients are asking you questions continually that give you more than enough content.

Alternately, if you are a fiction writer and belong to a writer's group, take note from the critics in your group. They are your support. They will be giving you constructive criticism that you can use to develop your work in the same way as above.

Is that Fear Monster creeping back in? Kick its butt. Remind yourself that you ARE the expert. Say it out loud. *I AM the expert.* Write it down three times on the lines below.

_____

_____

_____

Over 6 weeks, write down three questions you are asked in your profession, or asked about with your fiction writing. Write down your answers. They need only be dot points.

Week 1: Questions asked:

1. _____
   _____
2. _____
   _____
3. _____
   _____

Week 1: Answers given:

_____
_____
_____
_____
_____
_____

Week 2: Questions asked:

1. _____

2. _____

3. _____

Week 2: Answers given:

_____
_____
_____
_____
_____
_____

Week 3: Questions asked:

1. _____

2. _____

3. _____

Week 3: Answers given:

_____
_____
_____
_____
_____
_____

Week 4: Questions asked:

1. _____
_____

2. _____
_____

3. _____
_____

Week 4: Answers given:

_____
_____
_____
_____
_____
_____

Week 5: Questions asked:

1. _____
   _____

2. _____
   _____

3. _____
   _____

Week 5: Answers given:

_____
_____
_____
_____
_____
_____

Week 6: Questions asked:

1. _____
   _____

2. _____
   _____

3. _____
   _____

Week 6: Answers given:

_____

_____

_____

_____

_____

Now you have the beginning of your content. No more wondering about what to write. Look at what you have and rework it to suit you. You don't always need to recreate the wheel.

When you have gathered your information, you might find it a little daunting. Is that the Fear Monster creeping back in? Are you making excuses? Are you saying to yourself – I can't deal with this. It's all too hard. It's too much. When am I going to get time to collate all my information? When am I going to get time to write this?

NO Excuses.

The content you gathered is the framework for you, as the expert, to expand on. These are a part of your chapters. Go back and look at your mind map. You've already spent your working life living these chapters, growing them from the ground up. Step by step, chapter by chapter, you have created something that is authentically yours. People know when you are being truly you and if you are giving value. You will have your readers eating out of your hands. Look at the responses you have to your questions. It's all there for you.

This is your heart-centered work and you've been doing it for years. It is what makes you the expert. Don't reinvent the wheel and try to change what you already know and are doing. Don't sit around waiting for that to happen. Don't sit around waiting for the perfect moment to begin writing. Just begin. Begin by using your blog posts, your email content, your you tube videos, your staff meeting notes of questions and answers. Do some Facebook lives. Look at courses you have run. Are there similarities or differences you can write about? You've got it all in front of you.

The key to writing success is to look ahead and make your words relevant. Give your content a fresh new look so the reader can continually see value in your work. Tell stories throughout your book. This will personalise it for the reader. You most likely already have them as part of your audience on social media. Now you are backing yourself by writing it.

CHAPTER SIX

Make It Happen

"Choosing a goal and sticking to it – Changes everything." Scott Reed

Setting SMART Goals

So, you've kicked your negative mindset, you've made a commitment to yourself and your readers, you've drawn yourself a mind map, and have content. Now it's time to focus on your goals.

Goals aren't new. We learn how to achieve tasks and goals at school then into our working lives. We make them each day. By intentionally stating your intentions and affirmations daily, out loud, you are half way there to making and meeting your goals. Affirmations set intent, intent creates purpose, purpose leads to commitment, commitment ends with the goal being accomplished. In this case, the writing and publishing of your book.

Write down on the line below, MY GOAL IS TO PUBLISH MY BOOK.

_____

_____

State it out loud with full intent. Add it to your affirmations if you don't already have it.

Now it's time to set some SMART goals.

What are SMART goals?

There are 5 of them. SMART is an acronym that stands for:

Specific, **M**easurable, **A**chievable, **R**ealistic and **T**imely.

SMART goals are explicitly stated. They are clear tasks and accomplishments that are well defined and unambiguous. They can be measured against specific criteria that considers your progress towards the accomplishment of your goal. They are goals that are totally achievable. Each goal you set must be aligned with the five SMART criteria. If you do this, you will have a line to base all of your focus and decision-making thoughts on.

SMART goals are goals that are attainable, achievable. They are realistic. You know you can reach them no matter what.

Your SMART goals will look something like this:

I will write _____ words per day / week.

I will complete my first draft by

_____.

I will get my manuscript to my editor by

_____.

I will review and edit the content by

_____.

These are all SMART goals that you set for yourself to keep you on track. They aren't set in concrete but are there as a guide for you.

It can help to write a timeline for yourself. Pick a date when you think you'd like to see your

work published and work backwards.

For example:

- *June 2020:*   *No Excuses published.*
- *May 2020:*   *Add pre-orders to website.*
- *April 2020:*   *Finalise Cover Art.*
- *March 2020:*   *Format text.*
- *February 2020:*   *Complete Editor feedback.*
- *January 2020:*   *Editor.*
- *December 2019:*   *Edit second draft.*
- *November 2019:*   *Edit first draft.*
- *October 2019:*   *Complete first draft.*

By creating a timeline, you are reinforcing the commitment you made to yourself and your audience. Timelines are fluid, life does get in the way at times, but it is there as a guide for you.

If you have a support network, reach out to them. We all have days when the world is too much and we just want to curl up in fetal and rock in the corner. What do you do on these days? Turn to your network, your support systems, your tribe, your accountability partner. Whatever you like to call them. These people will always have your back. They are your inner circle, the ones you can count on to lift you up when you need it most. They understand you. They understand what you are going through. They understand that the Fear Monster might be raising its ugly head as those tiny thoughts of doubt creep into your mind. These people will help you attain each one of your goals as well as a positive mindset.

Write down the names of those people you consider to be a part of your network.

_____

_____

_____

_____

_____

_____

CHAPTER SEVEN

"Dream. Plan. Believe. Do."

Anon

Dreams Do Come True

Can you visualise holding your finished and printed book in your hand?

Yes?

I hope so.

Publishing a book is a dream regardless of whether it is to promote your business or to pursue creative endeavours. You may be a wonderful cook, or photographer and want to share your skills to the world. You may dream of romance, so you write about it. Whatever or whoever you write your story for, they are your audience. They will be there with you to celebrate you holding your book in your hands, and theirs.

Writing is, at times, a very solitary pass time. It's your journey and yours alone. My experience of writing a book will be very different to yours even though we ultimately have the same goal in mind – to get published.

Use your support network to help you build your audience while you are writing. While your words are still thoughts – ideas in your head. Your audience are your potential readers who will purchase your book. You have built a relationship with them; created mutual trust. They genuinely want to read your story.

Use your book at speaking events, conferences. Promote it and what you write on all social media platforms. Your book is you; it's your business, it's who you are. Your story gives you credibility as a published author and in business.

Let your dream become your reality. Stay positive. If you find yourself faltering, repeat your positive affirmations. Turn to your support network. You've got this!

Doing the quick 5.

On the following page, spend 5 minutes writing down 5 big dreams you have about being a successful author. That's one minute per dream. Do this as many times as you want or need to. Do not over think it. Put a timer on and stick to it.

Ready. Go …

1.

2.

3.

4.

5.

CHAPTER EIGHT

"Self-care is giving the world the best of you, instead of what's left of you." Katie Reed

Marketing and Self-Care

Committing yourself to not only writing your story but marketing it, comes with much self-care.

You can never start marketing your book soon enough. It takes time and effort to brand yourself as an author and to grow your audience. You need to be active on all social media platforms – Facebook, LinkedIn, Twitter, Instagram, Pinterest. You need to be blogging; tweeting, for example, guiding people to your website. Email lists and newsletters are powerful. Look out for speaking opportunities. Connect with people who are in the same business as you or write in the same genre. Connect with people who aren't in your business to broaden your networks. Attend conferences, appear as a guest on podcasts and, in turn, invite guests to yours. There is so much out there you can do to be seen and build trust with your audience as a writer. All this will position you as an expert in your field and will continually bring new clients your way. When it's time to launch your book, you've already got your audience therefore, your buyers.

Marketing yourself, your brand and your book can be very demanding so don't forget self-care. You must make self-care a priority commitment to yourself. Continually putting yourself out there is hard work. Its constant, emotionally draining, relentlessly exhausting at times. You also have a life that doesn't involve any aspect of writing.

Writing a book does take time and effort. Along the way you need to learn to look after you. Self-care can be something as simple as walking on the beach, sitting under the moonlight, or gardening, meditating; going to a coffee shop. Do whatever you need to do for you. These times are golden moments for writers. They are also good times to restate your affirmations if you wish too.

On the following page state three self-care rituals you are going to do for yourself each week. Make them a commitment you *cannot* sacrifice. Change the rituals when and if you need to. They need to be something that makes you feel good about you and something that helps you to move forward not just in writing but in your daily life. Consistency is the key for success.

Weekly Rituals for self-care

1. _____

2. _____

3. _____
   _____
   _____
   _____
   _____
   _____
   _____

I personally like to state positive affirmations before I go to bed each night and on waking each morning before I rise. These are especially helpful and calming to me if I've had a difficult day or am finding it hard to focus. Other writers I know like to perform daily gratitude and journal writing. Do what is achievable for you and makes you feel good about you.

Write your affirmations or words of gratitude down each day. State them out loud. Three times each. Let them flow into your subconscious. Change them each week for a month. Make doing this as a part of your self-care, a daily exercise just as you are making writing a daily exercise.

My Affirmations/Words of Gratitude

Week 1: Affirmation/Gratitude

_____
_____
_____
_____
_____
_____
_____
_____

Week 2: Affirmation/Gratitude

_____
_____
_____
_____
_____
_____
_____
_____

Week 3: Affirmation/Gratitude

_____
_____
_____
_____
_____
_____
_____
_____

Week 4: Affirmation/Gratitude

_____
_____
_____
_____
_____
_____
_____
_____

Week 5: Affirmation/Gratitude

_____
_____
_____
_____
_____
_____
_____
_____

The Keys to Success is establishing your Why, knowing it 100% and making a 100% commitment to yourself. If you've gone through this book step by step you will know what that is very clearly. If you've got this far you will have kicked all your fears and are no longer making excuses. You've made a commitment to yourself and your readers. You've completed a mind map to guide you, and also, a timeline. You know your content and your mindset had changed from I can't to, *I can*.

So now, it's time to begin.

NO Excuses.

Thank you to all my readers. To those of you who support me in my own writing.

This is for you. So many of you have a story within you.

Walk through this guide one step at a time.

Believe in you as I do.

Before you know it, you will be publishing your story too.

Thank you

ABOUT THE AUTHOR

When I create it's like the Sun's warmth touching my skin after a deluge of rain. I'm in my happy zone once again.
Lorna Kopp

When I make something with my hands, I know that only I could make it – no one else can create exactly the same way. When we allow the universe to flow through us our ability to create is limitless.
Renee Baude

These are two of my favourite quotes. Writing brings such magic to the world. It enables people to feel, think, come to life, ponder, smile. That is my goal as a writer.

Working in education, I learned to hone my writing craft whilst coaching and mentoring students and teachers. I still enjoy sharing stories in the classroom – it's wonderful watching children's eyes light up as they scan the pages from left to right – their smiles growing as they laugh at the words and illustrations trying to make sense of a fictional world.

I am the Founder of Daisy Lane Publishing and Creative Collaborations and successfully manage an online coaching course for writers – Mindset Challenges for Successful Authorship. I am a YMag Thought Leader/Change Maker, an Ausmumpreneur nominee and a judge for the ABIA Book Awards. I'm also a multi-genre author with a passion for mentoring, speaking, and publishing quality books, written from the heart, acknowledging that one story can empower many. I adore stories that are written with passion, inform and educate the reader, offering them hope and strength, courage and resilience to continue on their journey regardless of who, or how old the reader is.

I continue to write in differing genres every chance I get – one never knows when the magic will rise. When not writing you can catch me reading with a cat or two on my knee or playing with my dogs at the beach.

You can find me at

https://daisylanepublishing.com

Facebook: https://www.facebook.com/JenniferSharpAuthor/
https://www.facebook.com/DaisyLanePublishing
https://www.facebook.com/creativecollaborations

Twitter: https://twitter.com/daisylanepubli1

LinkedIn:https://www.linkedin.com/in/jennifer-sharp-90920b16a/

www.ingramcontent.com/pod-product-compliance
Lightning Source LLC
Chambersburg PA
CBHW050321010526
44107CB00055B/2337